T0156504

Total Heart Makeover

Danielle J Londeree

WestBow
PRESS
A DIVISION OF THOMAS NELSON

WestBow Press books may be ordered through booksellers or by contacting:

WestBow Press
A Division of Thomas Nelson
1663 Liberty Drive
Bloomington, IN 47403
www.westbowpress.com
1-(866) 928-1240

ISBN: 978-1-4497-1679-0 (sc)
ISBN: 978-1-4497-1681-3 (hc)
ISBN: 978-1-4497-1680-6 (e)

Library of Congress Control Number: 2011929580

Printed in the United States of America
WestBow Press rev. date: 6/28/2011

This book is dedicated to the Lover of my Soul, Jesus Christ, who has taught me that in all things, He is more than able to be my "all in all."

Contents

INTRODUCTION

I am consumed by the desire to know the Lord and His most intimate plans for my life! I am sick of settling for less and being scared to step out in faith, in love, and in hope. I do not want to remain in spiritual complacency, but want to be challenged to see beyond this world and focus on the next. I want to be refined by the All Consuming Fire, purified in the Powerful Presence, and loyally devoted to the Lover of My Soul. In essence, all I want is more of Him and less of me! In this study are the lessons I have learned—and am continually learning—from pursuing the heart of my Lord and replacing my heart with a "heart like His." I pass these lessons on to you. My prayer for you during this total heart makeover is that you would be so in tune with the Holy Spirit that your life becomes a beautiful hymn of praise. I also pray that the Lord would remove any hindrances in your life that keep you from experiencing Him on a deeper and more intimate level. A.W. Tozer wrote of his own spiritual journey in his book, *The Pursuit of God*. He ends the first chapter with this prayer: *O God, I have tasted Thy goodness, and it has both satisfied me and made me thirsty for more. I am painfully conscious of my need for further grace. I am ashamed of my lack of desire. O God, the Triune God, I want to want Thee; I long to be filled with longing; I thirst to be made more thirsty still. Show me Thy glory, I pray Thee, that so I may know Thee indeed. Begin in mercy a new work of love within me. Say to my soul, "Rise up, my love, my fair one, and come away."*

Then give me grace to rise and follow Thee up from this misty lowland where I have wandered so long. In Jesus' name. Amen.

1. WE ARE HIS

The Creator of the Universe wants to know you. Not only does He want to know you, but He wants to make you his daughter (1 John 3:1), a princess in His kingdom! And He chooses to love you in ways that you don't understand nor may you ever truly realize all that He already has done for you just because He loves you. Yet, He is GOD! Who are we that He should care for us? We are but dust of the earth compared to His glorious riches. I often ask myself the same question King David asks of the Lord in Psalm 8, "What is man that you are mindful of him?" So why are we here and why does God care so much for us? In Revelation we read that "Thou hast created all things, and for thy pleasure they are and were created" (4:11 KJV). Simply said, we were created for God's pleasure. I am confident He has some greater plan for which we were created, but regardless, we can confidently say that we were created to bring pleasure to the Lord. This means that the Lord takes pleasure in seeing us grow up, just like parents like to watch their own children grow daily. The Lord takes pleasure in blessing us. He takes pleasure in seeing us enjoy this earth. He celebrates life's greatest moments with us and rejoices with us. But most importantly, God desires us to come to know Him in an intimate way. This is what He takes His greatest pleasure in. I love how A.W. Tozer expresses biblical truths, so I tend to utilize his words often in this study. He states,

Let us keep always in mind that God also has desire, and His desire is toward the sons of men, and more particularly toward those sons of men who will make the once-for-all decision to exalt Him over all. Such as these are precious to God above all treasures of earth or sea. In them God finds a theater where He can display His exceeding kindness toward us in Christ Jesus. With them God can walk unhindered; toward them He can act like the God He is." [1]

God wants to walk with us? He just wants to "be himself" around us and bestow nothing but kindness on us? Yes, that is exactly what I think God intended. Remember Genesis chapter 3 where the Lord was walking in the garden hoping to hang out with his objects of pleasure, Adam and Eve. Then sin got in the way and has kept us from enjoying the perfection of that relationship with our Creator. We now face the consequences of their actions, but the relationship with the Lord is still available to us through Christ (John 14:6, Rom. 8:1-4). Just look at Leviticus 26:11-12 for example: "I will put my dwelling place among you, and I will not abhor you. I will walk among you and be your God, and you will be my people." God still wants to walk with us. We have just to want it and seek it. Do you feel close to the Lord or does a close relationship seem unreachable? Do you view God as the big unapproachable Being in the Sky or do you see Him as your best friend who is walking right beside you?

What words would you use to describe your current relationship with the Lord?

_____

_____

_____

Do you feel it possible to walk closely with the Lord? Or to walk closer than you are walking now?

_____

_____

_____

So what does it mean to walk with God? Well, what do you normally do when you go walking with someone, especially someone you really love? You hold hands. You talk. You listen to each other. You laugh together. You help each other over the hard parts of the path. You watch out for those stumbling stones. You might even stop and smell the roses together. In the same way, we too can walk in joyful communion with God.

What do the following verses say regarding how we walk with the Lord?

Psalm 73:23, 27-28

_____

_____

Isaiah 41:10

_____

_____

Micah 6:8

_____

_____

Let's look at some Biblical examples of those who walked closely with God. Is there anything that stands out to you about their lives?

Enoch: Genesis 5:21-24, Hebrews 11:5, 6

_____

_____

Moses: Numbers 12:1-8

_____

_____

Daniel: Daniel 10:12

_____

_____

David: 2 Samuel 7

_____

_____

Something these men have in common is their humble attitude before the Lord. They truly understood that the Lord is a great God and they are only His humble servants. That humility is the key to a closer walk with Thee. Do you feel distant from Him? Then humble yourself. Do you feel that He is not listening to you? Then humble yourself and get on your knees and pray. It is pride that gets in the way of our relationship with our Creator. Humble yourself accordingly. Read over Tozer's statement mentioned previously and notice when he says ". . . those sons of men who will make the once-for-all decision to exalt Him over all. Such as these are precious to God above all treasures of earth or sea." If we exalt the Lord and give Him the due respect He deserves and humble ourselves before Him, we will find favor with the Lord and we will be His children. So if you want to walk closely with the Lord, then get humble before Him; not only will He hear your call, but He will lift you up to Himself! James 4:10 says "Humble yourselves before the Lord and He will lift you up." 1 Peter 5:5 says that "God opposes the proud, but gives grace to the humble. . . . humble yourselves, therefore, under God's mighty hand, that he may lift you up in due time." Only in humility will we ever be close to the God of the Universe!

Look at Psalm 51. What type of sacrifices does the Lord takes pleasure in (see verses 16, 17)?

_____

_____

_____

What is a broken and contrite heart? A heart that humbles itself before the Lord and admits its sin to God. A heart that understands it is mere dust compared to the glorious richness of God. It is a heart that understands it is sinful, yet longs to be cleansed and purified by the presence of the Lord. This is what the Lord desires of us. Tozer also states, "Every soul belongs to God and exists by His pleasure. God being who and what He is, and we being who and what we are, the only thinkable relation between us is one of full Lordship on His part and complete submission on ours. We owe Him every honor that is in our power to give Him."[1] In other words, how can we weak little creatures try to be anything other than a humble servant of the Lord? Remember back to Micah 6:8? What does the Lord require of us? Nothing, but to walk humbly with Him. It's not much to ask, so why don't we do it? The following Psalms are full of praise and honor to our Creator. I enjoy reading through them, for they remind of the Lord's great power and the appropriate praise that is due Him. They remind me of how big God is and how little I am, yet the Lord considers me worthy to be in a relationship with Him.

Read through these verses and write down some of the phrases that really stick out to you regarding God's awesomeness.

Psalm 8

_____

_____

Psalm 29

_____

_____

Psalm 33

_____

_____

Psalm 104

I also advise that you read Job chapters 38 and 39. This is where Job questions God about his situation and God verbally answers him—with a hint of sarcasm—and reminds Job of who the Great I Am really is. In chapter 42, Job humbles himself and says, "I know that you can do all things; no plan of yours can be thwarted. You asked 'Who is this that obscures my counsel without knowledge?' Surely I spoke of things I did not understand, things too wonderful for me to know. . . . therefore I despise myself and repent in dust and ashes." In the end, God tremendously blesses Job. In summary, if we humble ourselves before Him, then God will lift us up into His arms of love. We can walk hand-in-hand with the magnificent Creator and be in communion with Him. I challenge you today that if you feel distant from the Lord, then search your heart. Is there pride dwelling there? Then get on your knees physically, lower your head, and pray before the Lord. Humble your heart before the throne and exalt the King of Kings.

PRAYER CHALLENGE: Pray specifically that God would reveal anything that is keeping you from having an intimate relationship with Him. Whether it is pride, fear, or little faith, pray that He will show you how to humble yourself and overcome whatever is keeping you from experiencing Him on a deeper level. Write down what the Lord reveals.

2. NEW CREATION

The old is gone. The new has come.
2 CORINTHIANS 5:17

Let's look at how the Word contrasts the *old* versus the *new.* Read the following passages and write down the differences between the old and the new.

OLD LIFE NEW LIFE

Psalm 40:1-3

_____

_____

Ezekiel 11:17-20;36:24-31

_____

_____

2 Corinthians 4:4-6

_____

_____

2 Corinthians 5:16,17

_____

_____

Ephesians 2: 1-10

_____

_____

Ephesians 4:17-32

_____

_____

1 Peter 4:1-3

_____

_____

Obviously, there are big differences between the old creation and the new creation. The old life lived in the slimy pit of sin. The old person did not honor God in body nor in spirit. The old heart was hard and cold. The old self was only concerned with the ways of this world. But we are new if we have come to know Him, the only true God. The new creation loves the Lord. The new creation has given up the life of sin. The new creation has a new song—new attitude, new heart— that is lifting up the Lord in praise. The new self is concerned about the Lord's affairs. The new heart is soft and tender, full of compassion. The new life is evident for all to see. It is a light in the darkness shining to give others hope. The new life has let go of the past and is focused on the glorious future awaiting those who have received Christ. Isaiah 62:2 and Revelations 2:17 even talk about the new creation receiving a new name. This is a name given only by God, not by our parents or friends. It is a name chosen specifically for us. It is God's secret name for us by which He may already be calling us. I believe that this name will give us the warm fuzzies when we hear it and will be a constant reminder in eternity that the old world is forever gone and that eternity with the Father is only the beginning.

How new do you feel? In other words, do you feel a big difference between your old life and your new life when you came to know Christ? On a scale from 1 – 10 (10 being a big difference and 1 being no difference) how would you rank your life? For those that were young when they became a Christian and don't remember the "before Christ" life, what about if you can notice a difference between five to ten years ago compared to today? What are some things that were part of the old life that you are still struggling to overcome?

_____

_____

_____

_____

Do you feel guilty that you haven't overcome any of the "old" struggles?

_____

_____

_____

_____

What are some things that were part of the old life that are not evident in the new life? (In other words, what are some things that have changed about your life?)

_____

_____

_____

_____

Our new lives are to be set aside for God. They are to represent Christ and be holy and blameless. We are not to continue in sins that represent the old life. Obviously this is not easy and we fail many times, but as long as we continue bringing these sins before the Lord, He will sanctify us and make us new. It is the Lord who will wipe away these struggles and change our hearts. Do not let sin eat away at your life as David did in Psalm 32.

What were the effects of David's apathy towards his sins and his procrastination in asking for forgiveness, and how was his heart changed once he had let it all out before the Lord?

Negative effects of Prayerlessness:

_____

_____

Positive effects of asking Forgiveness:

_____

_____

PRAYER CHALLENGE: If there are particular sins you are still struggling to overcome though you are now living the "new" life, this is the time to relinquish them up to the Lord and have Him change your heart and show you how to overcome them. Then ask Him for forgiveness and a new heart to overcome them. Ask Him to show you the way out of temptation when you struggle with them. Use the following area to journal what the Lord is telling you during this time.

3. Sanctify Me

Just because we are a new creation does not mean we instantly become holy. What it does mean is that we now have the power to overcome any of the sins we struggle with. It also means our slate can be wiped clean at any point of the day and we can be renewed. The new creation that we are will continue to struggle in sins related to our old self. And as we grow more Christ-like, we may add new sins to our laundry list that we didn't struggle with before (pride, judgmental attitude, etc). It will be a constant battle we will face until we die. So what should our attitude be? Should we sit in a state of depression over the fact that we will struggle with sin our whole life? Should we not try to become Christ-like? Won't we just keep failing? The answer is NO! That is not what God wills for us. He loves us just the way we are, but He also loves us enough that He doesn't want us to stay in the sad sinful state we are in. 1 Thessalonians 4:3 states that it is God's will for us to be sanctified (to become more like Christ, holy and set a part for God). One of His purposes in our lives is for us to be more like His Son. I believe sanctification is a two-fold process. It involves the working of the Holy Spirit in our lives as well as our obedience to the Lord. Without each part contributing, there will be no sanctification.

What do these verses say about God's active role in this process?

John 17:17-19

_____

_____

Philippians 1:3-6

_____

_____

Philippians 2:12,13

_____

_____

1 Thessalonians 5:23,24

_____

_____

1 Peter 1:2

_____

_____

The process of becoming Christ-like cannot occur unless we are conquered by the Spirit. What does that mean? Tozer says it nicely.

Well, no one can do it [replace the old self with the new] alone, nor can he do it with the help of others, nor by education nor by training nor by any other method under the sun. What is required is a reversal of nature and this reversal must be a supernatural act. That act the Spirit performs through the power of the gospel when it is received in living faith. Then He displaces the old with the new. Then He invades the life as sunlight invades a landscape and drives out the old motives as light drives away darkness from the sky. The way it works in experience is something like this: The believing man is overwhelmed suddenly by a powerful feeling that only God matters; soon this works itself out into his mental life and conditions all his judgments and all his values. Now he finds himself free from slavery to man's opinions. Soon he learns to love above all else the assurance that he is well pleasing to the Father in heaven.

In other words, when we realize that the gospel requires us to lay down our own life because Christ's death on the cross purchased it with the blood He shed, then we should be willing to give it up to the work of the Spirit. This giving of ourselves is the giving up of our Self (our pride). As we come to the Father in humility, the Spirit invades our hearts and minds and lives in us. This supernatural act of the Spirit is the first step toward being set apart for God.

The following verses describe our role in sanctification.

Leviticus 20:26

_____

_____

Hebrews 12:14

_____

_____

1 Peter 1:15

_____

_____

1 John 2:3-6

_____

_____

The Holy Spirit will tell us which way to walk (Isaiah 30:21), but then it is our turn to take the step in that direction. Don't be deceived to think that sanctification does not require us to participate. We must choose to obey; choose to be holy! We must choose to let the

Holy Spirit have our heart. For example how many times have I been hard-headed in an argument with someone. I cling to the anger because it feels good and justified, yet I know it is not the right attitude to have or the right way to behave. I struggle to give it up and so I fight in a tug-of-war match, refusing to let go of the rope. But once I decide to step aside and pray, and ask God to change my heart, it is amazing how quick my heart changes. Sometimes instantly I find myself apologizing or changing my response to the situation. God gives me a peace about it and works the situation out. The point is I can't expect the change to come unless I actively turn to Him in all situations. Obeying God and actively trusting Him in all circumstances is the second step of sanctification. Step by step we become more and more set apart for God's purposes.

What words describe the sanctification process in your walk with God? Is it a slow process? Is it a constant tug-of-war battle? Is it a daily occurrence?

Have you ever experienced a time when your heart changed because you stepped aside and gave your heart over to the Lord? Write down the details and thank the Lord for His active power in your life.

Name a recent time when you felt God calling you to step aside and obey Him in something, but you refused. How do you think

the situation would have been blessed if you turned to the Lord during it and allowed Him to change your heart?

_____

_____

_____

_____

PRAYER CHALLENGE: Ask the Spirit to invade your heart. Ask Him to conquer your old self and to fill all the rooms of your heart. Ask Him to show you the specific ways He is trying to sanctify your life.

4. Breaking the Cycle

How do we keep on going towards Christ when it seems so often that we keep falling down? How do we keep our relationship with God from looking like a crazy roller coaster, full of highs and lows and upside downs? How do we overcome habitual sins that keep coming back to haunt us? I think every woman struggles with some sort of cycle in her life, besides menstruation (smile). Maybe it is struggling with a certain sin that you seem to overcome for a little while, but then find that you are right back where you started. Maybe it is struggling with staying on fire for the Lord. Maybe it is just trying to have a consistent quiet time (devotional time) with the Lord. Whatever it might be, these cycles can be long-lasting and cause us to feel worthless in our relationship with God. We then feel like we can't be used by the Lord. My friend discusses her cycle and how she tries to overcome:

I started out on fire for the Lord as He was really moving in my heart and in my life. I changed so many of my former ways in order to walk closer to Him. I really transformed and matured over the course of a year and had a passion for living. I was so excited about what God was doing in my life. I was very optimistic and flying high on life. I found joy in the small things and realized how my priorities (of my old self) had been focused on things that weren't all that important. The Lord revealed so much to me during that time and He helped me change my life and turn it completely around. I focused more on Him and made Him a priority. Then I came down from this spiritual high and struggled with being *"hot"* one minute and *"cold"* the next in my relationship with the Lord. I noticed that I began to get caught up in the day-to-day tasks and routines. I was lacking joy in the small things that I had once been so grateful for. Although I had a daily quiet time (or tried to), I began just going through the motions. I was not having undivided attention to the Word and what the Lord was trying to teach me. I would get caught up in a busy, fast-paced lifestyle. When things seemed to be going along smoothly, I started depending less on God and more on myself. It took several spiritual *"wake-up calls"* before I realized how far I was drifting from God. The wake-up calls varied, but it was as if I had hit a wall where things started falling apart around me. I would get sick from wearing myself out with everything I was doing. I noticed I was more irritable and less optimistic. God was getting my attention and forcing me back on my knees. Finally, I would humbly pray to get back on track with God. After giving it all up to Him, I would open my Bible daily, pray whole-heartedly, and refocus on what really mattered. He would always change my heart and help me back on my feet again. Once again, I would feel the spiritual high that I had before. But the cycle continues and I battle it to varying degrees. I start out strong, but then I seem to run out of gas. What keeps me going is the reminder of God's promises to me. He extends a personal invitation to me that if I turn to Him, I will find rest when I am wearied and burdened from the labors and stress of this life (Matt. 11:28). He will be with me always; He will never leave me nor forsake me when I am struggling (Deut. 31:6). It is when I struggle that I realize I cannot do it on my own; I must rely on the Lord for strength as He makes up for all that I lack. His Grace is sufficient and His power made perfect in my weaknesses (2 Cor.12:9). I should delight in my weaknesses, hardships, struggles, persecutions, trials, and difficulties because it is through them that my faith is refined and strengthened (Jas. 1:2-4, 2 Cor. 12:10). The most difficult thing that I realized regarding this cycle is that my attitude is a choice. I can choose to praise God. I can choose to have a positive attitude about life. It is always difficult to struggle against my sinful nature, but I just have to recognize that God promises to provide a way out of temptation (1 Cor. 10:13). I have to choose the way. When you praise God with your mind, your heart will follow. Psalm 150:6 states, "Let everything that *has breath praise the Lord." It is God's faithfulness and promises that keep me going day by day. Even when I fall and stumble, He is always there to pick me up, dust me off, and get me started again in the right direction!*

Does this story seem familiar? How does it seem similar to your own walk with God?

_____

_____

_____

_____

Another friend of mine with this similar struggle of losing focus on Jesus said that she must "conscientiously choose throughout the day to abide in His love. I ask myself, *Are you choosing love?* Psalm 16:11 is one of my favorites for keeping me on track: 'You will show me the path of life, in Your Presence is fullness of joy; at Your right hand are pleasures evermore.'"

Henry David Thoreau states, "I know of no more encouraging fact then the unquestionable ability of man to elevate his life by conscious endeavor." In other words, we can change our lives dramatically just by adjusting our thought life. Maybe the cycle can't be broken in our lives, but should we stay in the pits of spiritual despair? Maybe it is impossible to walk on a spiritual high twenty-four hours a day, seven days a week, but should we sit in a state of shame and demoralization? What I have come to understand is this: it does not matter if the cycle breaks at all during our time here on earth. What matters is that we *choose* to get up and walk again. This is what it means to persevere. This is what Paul concluded after he prayed for the Lord to remove the thorn in his flesh and instead God's answer was that His grace is sufficient (2 Cor 12:9). Paul's issue (his thorn) did not get removed during his lifetime, but he still persevered in the faith every day with God's grace. He never sat in a pit of despair over it again.

Read Psalm 51 with a focus on verse 10. Look up steadfast in a dictionary. What does a steadfast spirit look like?

_____

_____

_____

_____

In this Psalm, David had just repented of his sins regarding Uriah and Bathsheba. In verses 7-12, you can see how he is pleading to the Lord to renew his heart and restore the joy of his salvation. Notice that David asked to be cleansed with hyssop. Why hyssop? This is the same plant used by the Jews to spread the Passover blood on their doorposts. It was also used in purification rituals detailed in the Law. While there is some debate as to whether this hyssop is really the hyssop of today or another plant commonly found in Israel, regardless, the plant represented purity and humility before the Lord. David was asking for complete purity and cleansing that the Lord Himself would perform on him.

Do you think he only made this plea once in his life? If you look at Psalm 25 (for just one example), I think you'll see some similarity in the repentance, cleansing, and renewal of his heart. We may have a constant cycle of sin we deal with because of our nature, but just like David, we can repent, be purified, and given a steadfast spirit (unwavering, firmly established, focused) to persevere until the return of Christ.

LIFE CHALLENGE: Look up and write down the following verses on note cards: Matthew 11:28, Deuteronomy 31:6, 2 Corinthians 12:9-10, James 1:2-4. Keep these verses on you throughout the day every day for a whole week. For instance, maybe keep them in your pocket, purse, in your palm pilot, or on your cell phone. Throughout the day, read through them. If you feel like you are struggling, then read them aloud and remind yourself of God's promises. And guess what? Eventually you will have them memorized, and the Lord will recall them to your mind when you need them.

5. MY ALL IN ALL

I really think that the key to following hard after the Lord and having a steadfast spirit is to truly believe that God alone will really satisfy you in life. He alone can fulfill all of our desires and can mend any emotional scars. He alone can fulfill any void in our life and truly be the Lover of our Souls. I think that as a woman, we sometimes have a hard time accepting this. We have so many "if only" ideas that we think will make us happy or give us purpose in life. If only I was married, then I would be [just fill in the blanks: happier, nicer, living as I had hoped]. If only I could travel overseas and meet new people and see new places, then I would be. . . . If only I could get that great job and make more money, then I could spend more money on things like. . . . If only I had children, then I would feel. . . . But our husbands, families, friends, successful jobs, and achievements will not satisfy all our hopes and expectations. All these things will let us down at some point in life. It is God alone who can fill that void in our life because He is the one who formed our hearts in the first place. He knows us better then we know ourselves. Of course we can find temporal happiness in things or situations, but these will not last through the valleys of life. We need to truly understand that everything we work for—money, accomplishments, success, happiness, etc.—is meaningless apart from God. Without Him, life will seem insignificant and at times, despairing; all of our striving for happiness will be in vain.

What do the following Psalms say about our hearts and how the Lord will satisfy us?

Psalm 16:2, 11

_____

_____

Psalm 33:13-15

_____

_____

Psalm 37:3-4

_____

_____

Psalm 63:1-8

_____

_____

Psalm 73:25-28

_____

_____

Psalm 103:1-5

_____

_____

Psalm 145:13-21

_____

_____

These Psalms have much to say about desires. A few phrases (changed to be more personal) that stick out to me are: • He fulfills my inner desires • He formed my heart • The Lord is near to me when I call on Him. • He satisfies me as with the richest of foods • God gives me a bountiful supply of good things • God is the strength of my heart • If I delight in Him, He will give me the desires of my heart.

In Psalm 16 after David says to the Lord "apart from the You, I have no good thing." The Lord responds back to Him, "The saints who are in the land, they are the glorious ones in whom is all my delight." That's right! The Lord delights in us. In Psalm 145 it says repeatedly that the Lord is loving toward His creation and good to all He has made. He who takes delight in His creation and loves them will surely not let them waste away with unmet needs. God will satisfy and fulfill our hearts, but there is a catch: we must remember it will be fulfilled in His perfect *timing*. Verse 15 of Psalm 145 says "You give them their food at the proper time." He is faithful to fulfill the needs of every living thing in the timing He thinks is best. Not in our own human and fallible timing, but God's perfect timing.

Why is it hard to believe/realize that God can satisfy us? What is it about a woman's heart that makes us not trust God in the matters of the heart?

_____

_____

_____

_____

Is there a particular desire in your life that you have a hard time giving up to the Lord? How are you trying to pursue it on your own?

_____

_____

_____

_____

I have a friend who struggles with the desire to get married. She has a fear that God will call her to be single and that all her hopes of romance, having children, and being a wife will not be fulfilled.

She is scared that she will be missing out on life without these things. I think this is a common struggle among single women. I believe we do feel a strong sense of purpose in being these things, yet, God will satisfy us if we relinquish our own desires for our lives and give them up to Him. He understands our hearts and our fears and as we give up worrying about these things and focus our attention on Him, He will never cease to give us great joy! Remember Psalm 37:4: "Delight yourselves in the Lord and He will give you the desires of your heart." This is the real heart of the matter. If you delight yourself in Him first, then all else will be given to you and He will fulfill those desires you have. This is a promise from the Lord. In A.W. Tozer's book, *The Attributes of God*, he states: *And yet we are not a happy people because we've got our minds set on things. We multiply things and we increase things and we perfect things. We beautify things and put our confidence in things and God. We have our jobs and God; we have our husbands and God; we have our strong body and God. We have our ambition for the future and God, and so we put God as a plus sign after something else.*[5]

The fact is if we give half of our heart to God and the other half to the "and", we will still be disappointed in life because the "and" is not going to satisfy us. The "and" will always let us down at some point. The "and" is not perfect and does not truly understand us, etc. But if we give God all of our heart and depend not on the other things to make us happy, He will satisfy. God promises that we are missing *no good thing* if we walk according to his commands (Ps. 84:11), so why are we not full of rejoicing at all times? Why are we thinking we need more of something to keep us happy? Tozer says "If there is anything necessary to your eternal happiness but God, you're not yet the kind of Christian that you ought to be, for only God is the true rest."

There are also new discoveries to be made when we let the Lord master our dreams. We may soon discover that what had once been a priority to accomplish now seems so unimportant. What was once so urgent to have and to hold, is now perhaps a fleeting memory. We may find that the Lord will give us new dreams and desires, ones that we never thought we would ever care about. That's just all a part of the Master's plan! He is always full of surprises!

When I was in college, all I thought about was all the places I wanted to travel to. I really thought that life out in the plains of Africa was much more exciting and fulfilling than living here in the States. I would even toy with the idea of "being called" to live a missionary life in Africa. On a summer trip to South Africa, I seriously thought about how I could move there and yet still somehow finish my degree at the University of Florida. I had fantasies about life in the wild, and I really thought that I would feel happier there. But God changed my heart.

It was not easy. I wrestled with Him over it. I would try to show God why I should live overseas. I would explain over and over again how much greater good I could do for Him over there than here. Then when I finally relinquished my dreams and accepted His plan for my life, my heart's desires actually changed and I started being passionate for people here. While I still love traveling, and Africa still holds a dear place in my heart, God gave me a glimpse of His plan and it filled me with passion for Him first and foremost. Then He showed me a ministry to be involved in, which happened to be located in my hometown. He also gave me a passion for encouraging women to grow closer to the Lord, and that is what gets me excited now. I never thought that I would be passionate about staying in the States to reach people for the Lord, but that is exactly how God has changed my heart. I also went through a time when I felt like I should seriously analyze my heart and its desires. I realized I was not trusting God to fulfill my desires, but trusting in a "life of adventure" to fulfill me. I now understand that God alone will fill me with His Spirit, satisfy my desires, and direct me to accomplish His purpose in ways that amaze me! That is the true adventurous life! Yet, there are times that I get caught up in the idealistic dreams of a more adventurous life. It is then that I pray for God to fulfill me instead. Most of the time He grants me an amazing sense of wonder at the work that He is actively doing around me. Then at other times, He does bless me with some opportunity to travel and have my "overseas adventure". Yet, it is He who works out all the details and I just sit back and enjoy the ride. Regardless of how He answers my prayer, He always satisfies me.

The same is true for my friend who struggles with the desire for a husband. While she tells me that it does not happen overnight, the Lord does begin to satisfy her as she devotes herself to prayer and the Word with passion and consistency. As she spends time with Him, He gives her peace and patience for the journey that He is taking her through. Now He can do the same for you in whatever you may be struggling with today.

PRAYER CHALLENGE: Make a list of the desires of your heart. Pray to the Lord about each specific one. Ask Him to either change your heart concerning it and to satisfy your heart with Himself or to fulfill your desire and give you the patience and peace to wait for His timing. Memorize Psalm 16:11: "You have made known to me the path of life; you will fill me with joy in your presence, with eternal pleasures at your right hand." Say this verse aloud whenever you pray about the desires of your heart.

6. THE SECRET OF CONTENTMENT

Discontentment with life creeps in when we don't get what we want. We want more money, more things, more time, more love, more respect, and on and on. Our hopes get shattered, things don't go our way, and we blame everyone else for our broken expectations. We may even blame God for not listening to us or answering our prayers in a timely fashion. Discontentment hardens our hearts and causes us to focus solely on ourselves. It is a very selfish emotion. But God knows what is best for us. He knows what things are good for us to have. For example, a baby cries because her toy was taken away from her. She wants her toy back and does not understand why she can't have it. What if the toy the baby wanted to play with was a knife or a bottle of bleach. Obviously as parents, we take it away and give the baby only good toys to play with, ones that will help in the development of the child and are safe for the baby to play with. The parent, who knows what is best for the child, purposely took away the toy because it is harmful and not good for the child to play with, but the child does not understand. The baby may struggle for years before understanding that the "toy" is not good for her, but some day she will understand (or we hope.)

I'm sure we experience this same thing with the Lord. We are His children and He disciplines us and trains us up into "spiritual adulthood." Yet, most of us act like babies, crying and complaining all the time. "We want it now," we cry as we flop around on the ground having our temper tantrum. It's a wonder that God never tires of loving us! We must remember that God gives us exactly what we need. He promises to provide only what is good for us. He is not going to let us play with those things that are not going to benefit us eternally. Psalm 84:11 states, "No good thing does he withhold from him whose walk is blameless." If we are growing in Christ and seeking His righteousness in our life, then everything we have or are going through must be good for us, even if we don't understand how or why. Proverbs also has a lot to say on why people are not content.

What do the following passages say is a key to fulfillment?

Proverbs 13:4

_____

_____

Proverbs 19:23

_____

_____

Proverbs 20:4, 13

_____

_____

Proverbs 21:17

_____

_____

Proverbs 22:9

_____

_____

Proverbs 28:20

_____

_____

Proverbs 28:27

_____

_____

In other words, sometimes there is more to getting your desires fulfilled than just delighting in the Lord. The Bible clearly says that contentment also requires faithfulness, righteousness, and diligence. My favorite saying from my father is, "You have to be bless-able in order to be blessed." If you are lazy and not working hard at whatever your hands find to do, why would God give you an abundance of rewards. You need to be diligent and hardworking first, then He will bless you. If you are greedy and do not support your church or the poor and needy, why would God bless you with an abundance to hoard for yourself. If you are seeking after wealth and riches to make you happy, why would God grant you that which would take your focus away from Him? I ask you to analyze your heart and see if there is an area of your life that is "un-bless-able." Yet, even if we are blessed by God and have all of our needs fully met, there are times when contentment just doesn't happen naturally. It is something that requires mental discipline.

What do the following verses say about the secret of being content in all circumstances?

Philippians 4:10-13

_____

_____

Philippians 4:19

_____

_____

1 Timothy 6:6-10

_____

_____

Hebrews 13:5-6

_____

_____

Charles Stanley says in *The Glorious Journey* that contentment is "accepting God's sovereign control over all of life's circumstances." He goes on to say that there are three truths we need to accept in order to be content (and these are backed up in Scripture by the verses we just read): 1) Contentment has to do with our inward thinking, it has nothing to do with our circumstances. It is an attitude of the heart. 2) The secret of contentment includes distinguishing between what you need and what you want. It means rejoicing over the promise that God has provided for all your needs. 3) Contentment is a matter of trust. It means trusting God even when things seem out of control.

In relation to the first truth, I am reminded of the book by Stephen Covey entitled *The Seven Habits of Highly Effective People.* The first chapter discusses a concept called "Proactivity." In essence it says that our behavior is a function of our decisions, not our conditions. Highly proactive people recognize that they have responsibility (response-ability, i.e. the ability to choose a response). They do not blame circumstances and conditions for their behavior. Their behavior is a product of their own conscious choice, based upon values, rather than a product of their conditions, which is based upon feelings. In contrast, there are also reactive people who are affected by their physical and social environment. If the weather is not good, they don't feel good. If people treat them well, they feel well. Reactive people are driven by emotions, by circumstances, and by conditions. Proactive people are driven by their values and beliefs. Covey goes on to state that we can all choose to be proactive people, and it is this trait that makes one a highly effective person, effective in whatever one wants to accomplish in life.

Much of this study emphasizes the fact that one can choose to think differently about their life, choose to act differently during trials, and choose to persevere till the end. How hard is this to incorporate into your way of thinking?

If you are a reactive person, how can you remind yourself of the power of choice? Can you choose today to be a proactive person?

_____

_____

_____

_____

If you were to become a proactive thinker, what would immediately change about your life?

_____

_____

_____

_____

PRAYER CHALLENGE: Write down the areas of your life that you are dissatisfied with. Pray about each one, asking the Lord to show you where the discontentment stems from. If it is from not being bless-able, ask Him how to be righteous in that area. If it is from having the wrong mindset, ask the Lord to change your heart. As the Lord answers you, write down your thoughts. Keep your responses from the Lord as a reminder to yourself.

7. TREASURE THE LORD

When we think of the word "treasure," most people probably think of pirates and large wooden chests filled with gold and pearls and jewels. By definition, the word treasure means something that is of highly estimated value, most often associated with things the world considers valuable—money, precious stones, jewelry, etc. But the word is also used to describe those things we which we personally highly value in our hearts. These things may be the same things the world values, but they are also personal things we value that others may not care about. They are those things that take a hold of our hearts (and our time and interests) and we devote our lives to them. These things may be items that moths and rust may attack or they can be people, relationships, jobs, food, etc. They are those things we hold dear to our hearts.

Read Matthew 6: 19-24. What treasures are you building up here on earth that will not last through eternity? Think about those things that you put a value on that are only for our temporary living situation on this planet earth.

_____

_____

_____

_____

What treasures are you investing in that will last through eternity? Really think about your time and money that is spent on what will be ultimately rewarded to you in Heaven.

_____

_____

_____

_____

_____

Now I am going to ask you a tough question. Did you mention your relationship with Him as one of your treasures that will last through eternity? Hmmm? So, do you treasure the Lord? Is your relationship with the Lord something you value and would fight for? Do you protect your relationship with the Lord like you protect your loved ones? I have come to realize that many times I treat God as merely a friend I talk to on a regular basis. There are many times I am not seeking the Lord as though He were treasure. It's sad, but true and I know I am missing out. Missing out on what you might ask? Incomparable riches of Himself!

How do the following verses describe the Lord?

Job 22:25

_____

_____

Psalm 12:6

_____

_____

Psalm 119:14-16

_____

_____

Psalm 119:72

_____

_____

Ephesians 3:8

_____

_____

The Lord Himself is a treasure, worthy to be sought after, worthy to be valued, worthy to be respected, worthy to be praised! I am reminded of one of my favorite praise songs entitled "All in All." It speaks about seeking after the Lord.

> *You are my strength when I am weak.*
> *You are the treasure that I seek.*
> *You are my all in all.*
> *Seeking you as a precious jewel,*
> *Lord to give up I'd be a fool.*
> *You are my all in all.*
> *Jesus, Lamb of God. Worthy is your name.*
> *Jesus, Lamb of God. Worthy is your name.*
> ©1991 Shepherd's Heart Music, Inc.
> Words and Music by Dennis Jernigan

The Lord is the most valuable treasure we can ever discover. Just as we view treasure as something that is valuable and will give us great satisfaction, so too will the Lord. He is a treasure we should desire and seek after with all our heart. We should be rejoicing that we have a relationship with God just like one rejoices with great riches (Ps. 119:14).

Is God your gold? Are you seriously seeking after Him as though He is your treasure? Read Matthew 13:44-46.

In this passage Jesus is using an analogy of finding hidden treasure to finding the kingdom of God. It is something so valuable that those who find it are willing to sell everything they have in order to purchase it. Yet, the kingdom of heaven is worth far more than what any man can purchase, and so Jesus is merely trying to relay to us the value of being in the kingdom. It is a treasure of which we will marvel at one day when our time comes.

The term "rich" is often used in describing how great and abundant something is. We use the term to describe desserts like chocolate cake that are so "rich" we can only take a few bites of. Its sweetness is too rich for our palates and so just a few bites is more than enough to satisfy our taste buds. It's this same term that Paul uses many times in his letters to describe the "rich" aspects of the Father.

In the following verses, what aspects of God are rich?

Romans 9:23

_____

_____

Romans 11:33

_____

_____

Ephesians 2:7

_____

_____

Colossians 2:2,3

_____

_____

God's glory is rich! God's wisdom and knowledge are rich! God's grace is rich! Isaiah 33:6 says, "He will be the sure foundation for your times, a rich store of salvation and wisdom and knowledge; the fear of the Lord is the key to this treasure." God is rich in all His character traits. Just as one bite of a rich chocolate dessert is enough to satisfy our taste buds, so is one bite of God rich enough to satisfy and fulfill us! Do you understand how rich the Lord is? Do you contemplate how rich He is in love for you? We can't fathom how much love He has for us, how much grace and mercy He shows us, how much wisdom is hidden within Him. All we can experience for now is just a taste. A little bite to satisfy our thirst. But oh how wonderfully filling that bite can be! It's enough for you and it's enough for me.

PRAYER CHALLENGE: Write down all the amazing character traits of God on a piece of paper or in your journal. Praise Him out loud for being the God He is and thank Him for the riches of His character. I also challenge you to seek out a study or book on the attributes of God and see what new things you can learn about our Heavenly Father.

8. THE THIRST QUENCHER

Do you thirst? Is there emptiness in your heart that longs to be filled? Let's look at the life of a woman who is really thirsty: the Samaritan woman by the well. **Read John 4:7-14 for the full story.**

Now here is a woman who has had her share of troubles in life. She has been heart-broken, not just once, but five times. I am guessing that she is the type of woman who finds her confidence in the attention of men. Maybe she also defines her worth by her beauty and her charm. Or maybe she thinks that her unhappiness is due to not having the right husband and that if she could only find Mr. Right, then all else would be resolved. Yet, these things have failed her, and she goes from one broken relationship to the next. I see her same struggles in many women today, and it saddens me greatly. With each new relationship, they take with them their baggage of hurts and disappointments. They just don't realize they can be free from all the despair they experience. So what does Jesus offer her? Something to fill the emptiness she has. But she tells Him that the well is deep. Her pain and despair are too deep for Him to heal. They go back to when she was a young girl. How can he possibly know the depths to which she has been hurt? How can he be any better than those who have come before him? Jesus goes on to say that His offer will not only fulfill her thirst for purity, for forgiveness, righteousness, and newness, but it will also make her own life a spring for which others can see the evidence of her faith and healing. Not only will she gain eternal life, but she will be like a tree planted by streams of living water, whose leaf does not whither. So she inquires more. She seeks the truth He is willing to offer. She wonders if what she is doing is right, for she currently doesn't feel like she is getting any favor from the Lord. Jesus answers that He is the Answer she has been waiting for. He is the Messiah. He is the one who can help her out of her emptiness and despair. So He shares with her that salvation is not about worshipping at the right temple location, but about the condition of her spirit. And while her spirit is searching for peace and understanding, Christ is right there ready to fulfill her. All she needs is to stop searching elsewhere! Stop searching for it in other people and start looking inside herself.

Now here is a little side note. The Samaritan-Jews had their own scriptures. They claim that they have the correct version of the Torah and that the Jewish Pentateuch is not the right one. Now we know that Jesus fulfills all the prophesies in the Jewish scriptures, but He also was fulfilling a prophecy in the Samaritan scriptures this day. For their scripture states:

There is a well of living water dug by a Prophet whose like has not arisen since Adam and the water which is in it is from the mouth of God. Let us eat from the fruit that is in this garden and let us drink from the waters that are in this well (Marqah, Memar 6.3)

And here comes Jesus as the Prophet, who is also the mouth of God which spews forth living water from God. This just amazes me. Why? Because Jesus met the woman where she was at. He not only physically went to her location, but spoke to her in terms that she would recognize. To me, this shows how much He loved her. And Jesus does the same for us. He doesn't want us to be perfect before we get in relationship with Him. He wants us right here, right now, right where we are at in life. Too many people think that they will come to the Lord when it's the right time or when they clean up their life. That's not what Jesus desires. He is ready and willing to be the living water in your own well of despair.

Is there any reason why you hold back from experiencing a closer relationship with God? Is there any reason you have yet to give Him your whole heart?

_____

_____

_____

_____

There are also many other Scriptures that describe the Lord as a source of living water. Look up the following verses and write down these phrases.

Psalm 36:7-9

_____

_____

Psalm 42:1,2

_____

_____

Jeremiah 17:13

_____

_____

_____

Not only is He described as living water, but there are other words used to describe Him. How do the following passages define Jesus?

John 6:35-40

_____

_____

John 8:12

Bread, light, and water are things essential to life. While all the people in John 6 were concerned about material items and miraculous signs, Jesus was telling them not to be focused on this world and their physical conditions, but on the eternal world and their spiritual conditions. As bread and water provide for our daily physical needs, Jesus provides for our spiritual needs. He is to be our *daily* spiritual bread and water! If Jesus came to give us abundant life and life to the fullest, then every time we seek life away from him, we are only shortchanging ourselves. I can get caught up in feeling unsatisfied with where I am in life: sometimes wishing for a more adventurous life in some remote country and sometimes wishing for a more peaceful life sitting on a porch swing. Sometimes I even get jealous of all the "adventurous" and "fulfilling" things happening in another person's life. It is then that I remind myself that every day with God is an adventure. Who knows where He will lead me if I give up all my own fears and desires over to Him? While He may or may not lead me to some remote country, He promises to fulfill me. Just as bread satisfies the hungry and water satisfies the thirsty, so shall my soul be satisfied with God! I know my cup of life will overflow with good things for He is my spiritual thirst quencher! The song "Breathe" describes this realization....

This is the air I breathe: Your holy presence living in me.
This is my daily bread: Your very Word spoken to me.
And I'm desperate for You.
And I'm lost without You.
©1995 Mercy/Vineyard Publishing
Words and Music by Marie Barnett

In less poetic form, this is saying that the Holy Spirit's presence living in my heart is the air I breathe (air is a constant necessity, without it I would die). God's Word is my daily bread spoken to me (my source of nourishment to keep me living)

Tozer sums it up very nicely:.....

For it is not mere words that nourish the soul, but God Himself, and unless and until the hearers find God in personal experience they are not the better for having heard the truth. The Bible is not an end in itself, but a means to bring men to an intimate and satisfying knowledge of God, that they may enter into Him, that they may delight in His Presence, may taste and know the inner sweetness of the very God Himself in the core and center of their hearts.[1]

Read Jeremiah 2:13. Have you dug your own cistern? In other words, have you trusted in your beauty or charm—or anything else besides the Lord—to fulfill you? Write down the cisterns you have been trusting in.

_____

_____

_____

_____

Realize that these are broken cisterns, ones that were never meant to hold water. If you don't store water in colanders, why would you store your most treasured possession and wellspring of your life (your heart) in things that were never meant to hold it?

PRAYER CHALLENGE: Memorize Psalm 1:1-3. Ask the Lord to make you just like that tree and make that the prayer of your heart every morning. If you have been waiting for the perfect time to give Him your heart, now is that time! Pray for the Spirit to cleanse your heart from sin, make you a new creation, and live inside you to guide you, protect you, and give you wisdom and understanding.

9. Focus Pocus and Meaningless Pursuits

One of my great pleasures in life is to take a run with my little girl, Julia. She holds tightly with both hands in her little stroller as I run on the cobblestone of the beach walkway. I do not use a jogging stroller, but opt for the $15 cheapy stroller to push her around in. I can tell by the looks that people think I should use the much safer, more sophisticated jogging stroller with large wheels that overcome any obstacle, perfectly designed for a jogging parent. But I argue that my $15 stroller is safe enough as long as I remain focused on the jog. Yet, if I lose focus and don't see the little divots in the road, then the $15 stroller doesn't do so well as I learned one Saturday. We were watching the surfers in the ocean that morning and I noticed a young boy surfing with his dad and I was trying to guess his age (I was amazed at how well he did at so young an age). As the surfers came up to the beach walkway, I started jogging back towards them, hoping to see the small boy and determine how old he was. As we passed by the place where the boy was, I turned my head to examine him and oops, the stroller hit the grass edge and went flying backwards. Then next came my tripping over the stroller and landing in the grass. Thank goodness my Julia has a strong grip and was strapped in! Embarrassed, I quickly got up to the remarks of the people who saw my mistake and headed back home feeling like a terrible mother who lost her focus on the safety of her jog with her little girl.

Focus is an interesting thing. It can make or break even the most well designed and thought-out plans. It can be the difference between winners and losers in every sport, every competition, and every battle ever fought. How often do we hear fathers telling their sons to "focus on the ball" instead of focusing on the pitcher? How often do parents complain that their children have lost focus in school and are not getting good grades. It's all about the focus.

So what do you focus on? Do you focus on the path laid out before you? Or do you look around and turn your head from right to left seeing what else is out there? When your focus is not directly in front of you, then where are you looking? If you are looking at everyone else's life then you are not focused on your own.

Read Psalm 73.

Written by Asaph, this psalm shows where Asaph's focus was. He was watching all those around him and it seemed to him that their lives were much better than his. They all seemed healthier and happier (the old phrase that the grass is always greener on the other side). Yet, none of these people were doing the Lord's will. So why should he? Maybe he would be happier if he didn't even have to deal with the Lord. But when he got alone with God and let all his emotions out, he got a glimpse of their destination.

What does he realize?

_____

_____

_____

_____

_____

As he humbles himself before the Lord, he realizes all that he has: the Lord is his portion, his strength, and his salvation. He changes

his focus from looking at what others have to looking at what he has in the Lord, and what he possesses is worth far more!

So now that you realize you need to only focus on the path laid out before you, then let me ask you a few questions:

Where are you going?

_____

_____

_____

_____

What are your goals?

_____

_____

_____

_____

Where do you see yourself in 5 years or 15 years?

_____

_____

_____

_____

More importantly, how are you currently spending your time in order to get there? Is it working?

_____

_____

_____

_____

Every year on January 1, I read back through some of my journals in order to help answer these questions for myself. I like to see how God answered prayer and helped me handle certain trials. I see how He changed my heart regarding some circumstances and how He changed others' hearts as well. I also see how far I've come in achieving any goals I made. I then analyze areas of my life that are fruitful and those that need to be pruned. It's a great time to sit still before the Lord and think a lot about my prayers and pursuits. God reveals a lot to me on that day. From being reminded of the work God is doing in my life and in those around me, to motivating me with passion for fruitful ministries, to revealing the wrong steps I took and how He corrected me. The number one challenging question that I analyze is "Am I living out my life the best I can?" To me, life is short, and we are only given one chance to live it, so I want to make sure I am using my life opportunity the best I possibly can. The book of Ecclesiastes was written by the wisest man who ever lived—Solomon (1 Kings 4:12, 29-34). As Solomon studied life in order to determine "what was worthwhile for men to do under heaven during the few days of their lives" (Eccl. 2:3), he realized that "everything is meaningless," a statement made over thirty times in this book. At first, that statement annoyed me. It seemed so despairing and I would wonder if it was worthwhile to attempt anything great in life. Yet, I have to look at the whole of what he is trying to say. I have to look at how he pursued his quest. So I read the whole book and learned much about life. Read the following verses to see how Solomon set out to discover the meaning of life.

Ecclesiastes 1:12-18

_____

_____

2: 1-11

_____

_____

_____

After all his study, Solomon then made the following conclusions:

2:24-26

_____

_____

5:10-12, 18-20

_____

_____

8:16,17

_____

_____

12:13,14

_____

_____

_____

Everything is meaningless apart from God. Without a relationship with God, all of our laboring and striving will be in vain. It is He who allows us to enjoy our life and to find satisfaction in our work. Money will not satisfy us, nor will pleasures of the eye, nor will all the men in the world. Our duty here on earth is to fear Him and keep His commands, for this will please Him and He will bless us and fulfill us.

Where would you be in life if you had no relationship with God or if living for God was just not a priority? What do you think you would be doing?

_____

_____

_____

In answer to this question, I always say that I would have probably ended up either as a struggling actress in Hollywood trying to make my way to the top by doing anything regardless of morals, or trying to make it as a model and most likely destroying my body by conforming to the world's standards of "beautiful". Desiring to be center of attention was one of my weaknesses when I was younger, and I know that without the Lord in my life, I would be doing whatever I could do to get on that center stage. But I have learned that those pursuits are meaningless, and now I have no desire for those things. God has changed my heart.

Is there anything in life you are pursuing that is meaningless?

_____

_____

_____

_____

To whom should we live for according to Colossians 3:1-3?

_____

_____

_____

Christ is our life! Without Him, we would surely die in this world of despair and pain and toil. Choose today to pursue what will last through eternity. First and foremost, choose today to follow hard after Christ and not let your focus be diverted to what everyone else is doing. Then choose today to remove the meaningless items from your life.

PRAYER CHALLENGE: Ask the Lord to show you the areas of your life that need pruning. Make a commitment to the Lord to remove these items from your life. These things may be as simple as not watching certain shows on television or listening to certain music or may be as big as not getting that degree you always

wanted because God has another door for you. Really listen to the Lord and lay aside your own desires. Why pursue something that will be meaningless in eternity?

10. What to Expect When You're Not Expecting

When my husband Don and I were engaged, we went to marriage counseling at our church. At the end of our last session with the counselor, she decided to share her own experiences/ disappointments in marriage. She told us about her bouts with depression during the first year of marriage that eventually turned into attempted suicide by driving her car into a tree. While she was recovering at the hospital, her husband asked her why she tried to take her own life. She explained that she was so unhappy in the marriage that she figured the only way out was to die. Her husband explained that he had no idea that she was not happy in their marriage. He thought their marriage was great, and it shocked him greatly to hear that she felt otherwise. When she recovered, they decided to go to counseling. What she learned from counseling was very surprising to her. She learned that what was really wrong was her expectations. She had put so many expectations on the marriage and on her husband that when they failed her, she became depressed. In other words, the depression was only a symptom of the real problem.

After our counselor shared this, I realized that this should have been shared in the very beginning of the counseling! We had talked about communication, arguments, money, and sex during the other sessions, but never about what our own expectations of marriage were. Needless to say, Don and I laid out our expectations on the table for each other to view, and we analyzed whether they were appropriate or not. It really helped us overcome many potential disappointments. While the other topics are important as well, I have found that expectations can be just as important, if not the number one thing people should discuss before they get married. I have known too many women who view marriage as this fairytale like dream where their husband will joyfully come home from work, immediately give his wife a passionate kiss, sit down to eat the dinner she gracefully prepared, compliment her throughout the entire evening, do the dishes after the meal, and then prepare her a bath with scented rose petals. Now I am not saying this can't happen, but wake up to reality if you expect it to. From the time we are little girls, we dream about our weddings and the husband who will sweep us off our feet. We like the whole concept of marriage because it makes us feel loved and we get to show the world that someone loves us so much they want to be committed to us for life. Our hearts melt if we see the groom crying over seeing his bride walk down the aisle. We love it when the groom shows the tenderness of his heart by speaking vows of love. We "ooh" and "ah" over each gentle touch he lays on her cheek while he kisses her. Then we look forward to our day when our own knight will do the same. Yet, there is a hidden danger lurking in our thought process and somewhere by the end of the "chick flick" we just watched, we have built an expectation on what marriage will be like for us.

So are expectations wrong? Shouldn't we expect certain things out of life and from God? Aren't we supposed to hope in the Lord? What's the harm in expecting things? Lets look at the definition of hope. Hope and expectation are synonyms, so I'll use them interchangeably. According to Webster, hope (noun and verb forms) is:

1) (noun) the feeling that what is desired is also possible
2) (noun) a person in whom or thing in which expectations are centered
3) (verb) to look forward to with desire and reasonable confidence
4) (verb) to believe, trust, and desire

The Bible is very clear on where our hope is to be placed. If our hope is based on anything but God, we will be disappointed. What do the following verses say concerning in what and what not to hope?

Psalm 25:1-3

Psalm 33:16-22

Psalm 130:5,6

Isaiah 40:27-31

Lamentations 3:25

So it's not that we shouldn't hope or have expectations, it's a question of where do our hopes lie. Are we trusting in the Lord to fulfill our desires or are we trusting in certain people to fulfill us? Are we doing things in our own strength and confidence, or are we leaning on Jesus? And if we are fully hoping in the Lord, do we have an expectation on timing? Are we expecting our answer to prayer right now or do we want God's best timing?

Let's look at a Biblical example of when expectations have gone wrong: Abraham and Sarah in Genesis 15 and 16 were told by an angel of the Lord to expect a child. While they were right to expect that the Lord will fulfill His promise, they expected it to be in their own timing. When things didn't work out in their timing, they felt like they should intervene and just help God out in fulfilling His promise. Their actions created the chaos that we are still experiencing today between Jews and Arabs. We can have wrongful expectations on the outcome of our prayers, the timeliness of God's response, the results of certain actions, and our relationships with others. One personal lesson I have learned is that life is a whole lot easier when you don't put expectations on people, places, or things. While I do put my hope in the Lord, I try not to have a specific expectation as to how or when He is going to answer my prayer. This allows me to sit back and enjoy the ride. I can be content in whatever the circumstance because I trust in the Lord. Proverbs 3:5-6 says to "Trust in the Lord with all your heart, lean not on your own understanding; in all your ways acknowledge Him and He shall direct thy paths." In other words, trusting in the Lord means that I have to give up my own understanding of the situation and just let God work.

PRAYER CHALLENGE: *Write down any wrongful expectations you have lately put on people, places, and things. After writing them down, go through each one with the Lord and ask Him to remove this expectation from your heart. Ask Him to fill you with peace over each situation. Memorize Proverbs 3:5-6 or change the words to make it your own prayer of commitment: I will trust the Lord with all my heart. I will lean not on my own understanding, but in all of my ways, I will acknowledge Him and I know that He will direct my path.*

11. Desire to Be Beautiful

In his book, *Wild at Heart,* John Eldredge talks about three desires that are common in a woman's heart: 1) To be fought for, pursued, wanted, longed for 2) To have an adventure to share, to be part of something grand 3) To be found beautiful, not just in a physical sense, but to be found captivating in who she is. I have pondered long and hard about the things Eldredge is saying, and I noticed that there is an order to it, that these desires are related to each other and are part of our subconscious thinking process. First, there is something in us that makes us want to be found beautiful in both the physical sense and in who we are. If we are considered beautiful, then we will be desirable and wanted and perhaps many will fight for us. Subsequently, if we are desirable, then we will find that person to share the adventure of life with us. Then we will know what it means to be loved.

Do you agree or disagree with these three desires? Have you experienced these in your own heart?

If you could add more to the list, what would you include?

_____

_____

_____

My own heart has these same desires. I have to admit that it does make my heart content and happy to know that my husband finds me desirable (isn't this what makes us dress up in fancy lingerie?). And when he confirms to me that he thinks of me as beautiful, my heart feels at peace and I feel special. His protection of me makes me feel loved and valued. I know he would not only fight for me, but would give his life for me, and this makes me feel loved. I look forward to sharing our "adventurous" life together, and I can enjoy it anxiety free because I know he loves me. For me, I agree with what Elderedge is saying. Admitting this opened my eyes to what I truly long for inside my heart—my longing to be beautiful.

First, let's examine what beauty is. Look up the word "beautiful" and "beauty" in the dictionary and write down its definition.

_____

_____

_____

_____

I noticed something very interesting when I listed the words describing beauty. My favorite phrase is "the quality that is present in a thing or person giving intense pleasure or deep satisfaction to the mind." I also noted words like "attractive," "full of grace and charm," and "something excellent of its kind." What I found interesting is how my preconceived idea of beauty overshadowed what beauty really is. I often think of beauty as only merely something that looks pleasing to the eye. I think the media, and the world for that matter, often think of physical perfection as the only definition of beautiful. When I first thought of the term "beautiful," I thought of movie stars that I think are physically gorgeous. But isn't it interesting that "beauty" is not really defined that way?

I have come to realize that there is so much more to characterizing a beautiful person. Let's look at what Scripture says about beauty. If you look up the word "beautiful" in a concordance, you will find that Scripture talks about many women in the Bible as beautiful. The list of women includes Sarah (Gen 12:11), Rebekah (Gen 24:16), Rachel (Gen 29:17), Bathsheba (2 Sam 11:2), and so on. In these passages, it seems to be used to describe only physical appearance. Yet, I was never able to find that their physical beauty was rewarded in any way. They did not receive any special recognition in heaven for their appearance, and some of them are noted to have misused their beauty instead of using it to please their husbands. Physical beauty is not to be used for grabbing the attention of men or for deception, etc. There are plenty of verses in the Bible that warn against us misusing our physical beauty.

What do these verses say about misusing your beauty.

Proverbs 6:23-26

_____

_____

Proverbs 11:22

_____

_____

Proverbs 31:30

_____

_____

In other words, let us not be like the wayward woman who uses her charm and beauty to sway men to herself. Let us show discretion and be modest in our dress and with our words. I do like *The Message*'s paraphrase of Proverbs 11:22: "Like a gold ring in a pig's snout is a beautiful face on an empty head." In other words, beauty without being properly used with discretion is totally worthless and unattractive. The gold ring in the pig's snout does not make the pig look any better, its still an ugly pig.

So, for what are we to use our beauty? If you ever get a chance to read through the book Song of Solomon, I think you will agree that our beauty is to be used for our husbands. The word "beautiful" is used many times by the Lover (Solomon) to describe his Beloved and when reading the verses, you can tell he thoroughly enjoys her physical beauty.

One thing I did find in Scripture is that there is special recognition/rewards for those who display what I call "traits of beauty." These traits of beauty start the internal beautification process that will lead to our external beautification.

When I was in college, there were some women that I had come into contact with that I desired to be more like. They had something that I felt I didn't have, but I desired it. I searched and analyzed my heart and tried to figure out what it was. Then I realized that I would describe them as "beautiful" and "graceful" in talking about them to other people. It's not that they were on the covers of magazines or being mobbed by men asking for dates every night of the week. I felt like they were beautiful in a way that I wanted to be. Then I realized they were what the Bible describes as having true beauty. There were things about their character, the way they handled themselves in certain situations, the way people of both sexes respected them, and the way they displayed confidence that made me really admire them.

We often hear the cliché that beauty is only skin deep. The more I think about beauty, the more I realize how beauty and attractiveness are much more related to a person's inside than their outside. How often do we first meet someone who we think is beautiful or extremely good-looking. Then, once we get to know that person, we see their flaws (not their physical imperfections, but their "personality flaws") and then we wonder why we ever thought them attractive in the first place. The same is true in a male's mind (though they may not all admit it). I know many men who had found a certain woman very attractive. However, they witnessed her handle a particular situation where she acted extremely selfish and rude to the people around her instead of full of grace and peace. The men realized they did not want to be with her anymore and most of them switched from describing her as "beautiful" to something derogatory. In other words, beauty is definitely more than skin deep. I also read a survey in a magazine where they asked men what things they find attractive about women in general. The number one answer was confidence. All the other answers had to do with physical things like great legs, nice shoulders, etc., but the number one thing they found attractive was when a woman displayed confidence in herself. Interesting!

What specific traits of beauty are found in these Scriptures?

Proverbs 31:10-31

_____

_____

Matthew 26:6-13

_____

_____

1 Peter 3:1-6

_____

_____

In Proverbs, the list of traits is very long. The Proverbs 31 woman is truly amazing and there are many books written about her. Several characteristics stand out from this passage:
- she does not procrastinate, she works hard
- she shows discretion in how she spends money
- she shows compassion for the poor
- she provides care for her children

- she displays strength and dignity
- she has wisdom and a good sense of humor by not worrying about all the "what ifs" in life.

In Peter, the traits include:
- submission to her husband
- discretion in dressing (not putting value on appearance or dressing provocatively)
- free from worry
- gentleness of spirit

The trait of beauty in Matthew is simple: to show honor to the Lord.

Now in this world we live in, we are surrounded by the world's picture of bodily perfection as being the very definition of beauty. More and more people each year are undergoing cosmetic surgeries in order to become what they have always thought they wanted to look like. In the newspaper one morning, I found some very scary statistics on this trend occurring in the US on young girls age *18 and younger.* In 2003, there were 126,327 girls that received chemical peels; 42,515 girls received a nose reshaping; 39,921 had laser hair removal; 15,973 had their ears reshaped; 5,606 had Botox injections; 4,094 had collegen injections; 3,841 had breast implants; and 3,017 had liposuction. [2] And all of these girls are barely even adults! In 2003, American's spent over $1 billion in Botox injections alone, over $857 million was spent on breast enlargements, and $67.5 million was spent on just reshaping ears.[2] In 2004, there were 9.2 million cosmetic procedures performed, an increase of 24 percent since 2000.[3] I bet the statistics today would be even more staggering. Why are we obsessed with seeking perfection? In my opinion, it all comes down to people searching for happiness. The world is constantly searching for happiness away from the hand of Christ. It's the trend of trying to become desirable and beautiful so we can get that happy life we have always dreamed about. But when people still aren't happy after cosmetic surgery, what do they turn to? Sadly, new findings are showing a high suicide rate of women who get breast implants. According to Doctor David B. Sarwer from the Center for Human Appearances at the University of Pennsylvania . . .

To be honest, I don't think we know the exact reason why these women have a higher rate of suicide, but its very possible that a small minority who come in for breast augmentation are trying to solve significant psychological problems. I think some women come in with unrealistic expectations, that this surgery will make them more popular, get them the promotion they haven't gotten, or save a failing marriage.[4]

I feel there is some truth to this statement, for how many of those contestants on reality television shows like "Extreme Makeover" and "The Swan" complain about their relationships and broken expectations in life, as though if they looked better, all these things would disappear.

Do you agree with the statement made by Doctor Sarwer? Why do you think there is such a large trend of plastic surgery going on in America?

_____

_____

_____

I can't help to admit that watching these shows (even just periodically) and being bombarded by the media's definition of beautiful does take its toll on my perception of myself. I start to question my looks and to compare myself with other women. I have learned that this is a dangerous thing. It can lead to a spiral downward of self obsession in my looks if I don't catch it and take it captive to Christ. So how can we prevent ourselves from getting caught up in this snare? Some ideas:

- Memorize the traits of beauty as found in Scripture (or better yet, memorize Proverbs 31 or 1 Peter 3). Use these verses to combat against the temptation to obsess with the way we look.
- Write out 1 Samuel 16: 7 – "Man looks at the outward appearance, but the Lord looks at the heart." Put it somewhere on the mirror you use most frequently.

- Take every negative thought about yourself and analyze it according to God's standards. Remember that it is the Lord who made you! He formed you in the womb.
- Don't input into your mind the shows and images that are causing you to analyze yourself and make you feel inadequate. I know its hard not to watch a favorite show, but if its causing you to have low self-esteem, then its not good for you!

Do you have any other ideas on how to emphasize true beauty in your life instead of the world's idea of beauty?

_____

_____

_____

_____

Now I know I am going to step on some toes, but read Psalm 139 and consider the following: **Have you ever thought that by changing your physical appearance you may be complaining about the way God formed you?**

_____

_____

_____

_____

I am not saying it is wrong to get plastic surgery, but I am questioning the motive behind getting it done. Our hearts really need to be analyzed when we get caught up in the way we look. If you are contemplating cosmetic surgery, I think you should analyze what your expectations are first and determine whether they are realistic. Talk with other Christian women who can encourage you in the step you should take. Most importantly, pray about it. Don't think that God doesn't care about whether or not we get liposuction. He cares about every single aspect of our lives and He wants us to bring all of our concerns to Him for guidance. He is the first person we should be talking to regarding how we feel about ourselves! I will end with Psalm 50:2. "From Zion, perfect in beauty, God shines forth." In the Bible, Zion is the city of God that is considered the perfection of earthly beauty. Tozer has this to say about it:

Why was Zion the earthly perfection of beauty? Because her beauty came from the shining God who dwelt between the wings of the cherubim. She was not only architecturally beautiful but all the concepts of her were beautiful. Her hymnody was beautiful. Her ideas of worship were beautiful, shining there in the sun. . . . she was beautiful above all the earth. All things as they move toward God are beautiful. And they are ugly as they move away from Him.[5]

The same is true for us. As we move toward the Lord, we will indeed become more beautiful!

PRAYER CHALLENGE: Make a list of things you don't like about your physical appearance. Offer up your body as a living sacrifice to God in prayer and then burn the list (or throw it away in a symbolic manner) in order to show that you are truly offering it up to the Lord. Make a commitment to the Lord that you will not complain about these things, but will choose to focus on the eternal: our heavenly homes full of perfection.

12. Women of Worth

How do you see yourself? How do you think others see you? When you look in the mirror, do you notice all your flaws, whether they be physical or internal? Do you see a cowardly woman who is fearful of life's next bend in the road or do you see an overly confident woman who trusts in her beauty to help her win friends? Or maybe you see a woman who is tired and worn from the demands of life and looks like she needs a vacation. Or do you see a woman who seems perfect on the outside, yet you hope no one can see the mess she is on the inside?

Write down any words that describe how you see yourself (and how you think others may see you).

_____

_____

_____

_____

It is important to recognize that proper self-esteem comes from a proper relationship with the God of the Universe. You must first recognize how *valuable* you are to God. Why are you of value? Because you are first and foremost His object of pleasure (Rev. 4:11). Remember back to the first chapter. We were created to bring pleasure to the Lord. God actually delights in you and He is making you into a princess for His kingdom. Not only that, but lets not forget that He loves you so much that He sent His son to die on the cross for you (Rom. 5:6-8)! If the Lord did not value you in any way, He would not have sent Christ to die for you. That is what you need to recognize: how much you are loved by God. And once you recognize this, then you can humbly accept the offer to walk with Him who cherishes you. Second, you are God's workmanship (Eph. 2:10). You are precious to God because He is constantly working in you to do good things through you. He created not just your body, but your heart and soul as well. He created your inmost being! He knows you better than you know yourself!

The following passages utilize the analogy of a potter and clay to us and the Father. What conclusion can you draw?

Isaiah 29:16

Isaiah 45:9-12

Isaiah 64:8

Jeremiah 18:1-6

God never makes two pots alike, for each pot not only brings Him pleasure, but each pot is being made to serve a specific purpose. One pot might be used for watering the garden, another pot to keep oil, another pot to keep flour, and yet another to store cookies. We might not understand completely how the Lord is using us, nor might we see direct results of His work, but it doesn't mean we aren't being used for His purpose. I am sure that when Paul was in jail, he was thinking that he would be much more productive out in society sharing the gospel. Yet, he had no idea that the letters he wrote while in jail would end up reaching generations of people around the whole world! And so it is with you. God is using you in amazing ways, but you might not see the results during your time on earth.

As a side note, another conclusion we can draw from the analogy of the potter and the clay is this: how can we complain about our lives or ourselves when it is the Lord who is doing the molding and shaping in each of us? Can the pot talk back to the potter? We need to understand that the Lord is shaping us into the character of Christ on a daily basis. Each one of us is also a part of the Body of Christ, the Church. Just as our physical bodies have many parts that operate together to function, so does the Body.

How do the following verses describe you as a member of the body of Christ?

Romans 12:3-8

_____

_____

1 Corinthians 12:12-30

_____

_____

Maybe you are the eye or the hand or foot! Or maybe you feel like you are a part of the body that is weak and feeble—like a pinky toe— because you don't see mountains moved in your presence. Nonsense! First Corinthians 12 says that these "unnoticeable" parts are actually indispensable to the Body and you may be that part! You were given special gifts and skills to use for God's glory! If you don't know what these might be, I encourage you to find a study on spiritual gifts or talk with your pastor. Many of them have tests to help you see what gifts you might have. Also, look at the things you do well. Maybe you are good at finances, or teaching, or cooking, etc. No talent is too small to be used for God's glory. Pray to see where God might want you to use your talents; even those you might think of as trivial God can use in mighty ways! Remember that you are God's workmanship, created to do good works which God prepared in advance for you to do! So let's do them and stop complaining about how worthless we feel! It is when you are using the gifts God has given you that you will feel confident, knowing you are being used by the Lord.

Do you feel that you are precious to God? Why or why not? Read Psalm 139. How does this passage encourage you?

_____

_____

_____

_____

When I start to feel down, I have gotten into the habit of asking the Lord to send me a reminder of love for me—just a little something personal to give me encouragement. I know it might sound silly, but it is at these moments that the Lord sends me a little something to let me know He is there. Now He knows I love butterflies, and wouldn't you believe it, He often sends me one. It seems to come from nowhere to flutter around me. I consider them my flutters of joy, and they have become my personal little reminder that God thinks I am precious. At other times, He uses people to give me encouragement or will give me a verse to read, etc... But I must say, I do love the little butterflies delivering God's love to me. In the same way, ask the Lord to send you a personal reminder that you are precious in His sight. So in conclusion, we should realize our worth because of the following truths:

We were created for God's pleasure.

We are God's workmanship, created to do good works.

We are part of the Body of Christ.

PRAYER CHALLENGE: I encourage you to take one of the verses we covered in this section and memorize it. Take some time to sit

before the Lord and ask Him to reveal to you His love for you. Ask Him to also show you specifically how you can be used by Him. He who made you has many plans for you!

13. THE GARDEN OF THE HEART

I love to garden.
There is something about being outside in the fresh sunny air and working with my hands that makes me feel at peace. I also feel productive because I can actually see the fruits of my labor grow and blossom from little seeds. It's an amazing thing to see, but it also requires constant care. For example, there is a certain plant that keeps appearing in my pots. I never planted it there, but it seems to have found a home in my vegetable pots. The plant is a spiny fern. (It's incredible to me that some people actually buy the plant to stick in their yard!) Not only is it built to never die (it holds an amazing amount of water in its root bulbs so it can last through the longest drought seasons), it also has a root system that forms an incredible subsurface mat and unless you can physically remove all traces of the roots, the fern will keep coming back. In addition, the fern is rather prickly and requires a proper pair of work gloves to handle! Oh how I hate this plant! I have to constantly battle this weed in my yard and I have gotten to the point on many occasions where I feel I am fighting a hopeless battle against the spiny fern. But I keep on working at my garden because I know that my reward will pay off. Every time I taste a cucumber or lima bean or pepper, I know my labor has not been in vain.

In the same way, I view my heart as a garden. It is a garden that needs tender care and constant maintenance. I can plant many different types of plants in my garden of the heart, but not all should grow there and not all will have lasting fruit. If I plant good seeds and nourish them with the living water of Christ, then out of my heart will grow good fruits. If I plant evil or negative things, then out of my heart will grow these same things.

What do the following verses say about this?

Galatians 6:7-10

_____

_____

Matthew 12:33-37

_____

_____

As the gardener of the heart, we need to be constantly caring for the garden by weeding and removing any pests (mold, bugs, snails) that will cause damage to the plants.

So what are the good seeds to plant and what are those weeds that we should be destroying?

Good Seeds Bad Weeds/Pests

Psalm 119:10-11 Matthew 6:31-34

_____

_____

Proverbs 2:1-11 Mark 7:14-23

_____

_____

Proverbs 3:3 Ephesians 4:17-32

_____

_____

Galatians 5:22-26 Philippians 2:3,4

Philippians 4:8 2 Thessalonians 3:6-13

---

1 Corinthians 13 1 Timothy 6:10

Weeds are unwanted plants that grow up in our beautiful flower beds and vegetable gardens. They can grow unnoticed for a long time until they begin to choke out the good plants by sucking all the nutrients from the soil. In the same way, we need to examine what things we are letting grow in our hearts that are not good for us, things that may be choking the life out of the good things in our hearts. Do we let anger and jealousy grow in our hearts instead of planting forgiveness? Do we get caught up in allowing ourselves to worry and be anxious about what tomorrow may bring? Do we not mind the laziness and procrastination that waste our day? Do we let ourselves get caught up in gossiping about others? What about envy and boastfulness? Am I stepping on any toes here?

The world constantly bombards us with how we should be acting and feeling and telling us where our priorities should be. We need to take these things and filter them before letting them affect our hearts. Realizing that a certain action or thought is not Christ-like is the first step. The second step is to ask the Lord to remove it from our hearts. The third step is to prevent that same thing from re-rooting itself by not focusing on it. This means to stop thinking about it. For example, you might think it so innocent and harmless to think about someone else's husband, but you are only planting the seeds of destruction if you allow yourself to keep thinking about it. Immediately, when we realize it is creeping into our hearts, we must grab a hold of it and take it captive to Christ (2 Cor. 10:5). He will help us banish it from our hearts.

Are there any particular bad weeds that need to be uprooted from your own heart?

_____

_____

_____

_____

So how do we plant good seeds: the plants of wisdom, love, faithfulness, self-control, discernment, understanding, patience, etc.? First, as Psalm 119 said, we need to plant God's Word in our hearts! Then we can focus on trying to only allow good things into our hearts, things that are true, praiseworthy, noble, and pure. We should be asking ourselves if a thought or action falls in any of the categories of Philippians 4:8. If it does, it is worth doing, but if not, then we should not waste our valuable heart on it. I use this test to determine what I should be watching on television or in the movies or what I should be reading, etc. I often ask myself the following questions: Is it pure (godly)? Is it admirable? Is it right? Is it praiseworthy? This helps me narrow down what I should be spending my time on. It can be a hard sacrifice to tear myself away from a show that I view as entertaining, yet I have to remember that it may also plant weeds in my heart. When I decide that I am going to use that time instead to "set my heart on things above" (Col. 3:1-3) and things that will be good seeds, then God sometimes blesses me with experiencing something really neat that I wouldn't have ever experienced unless I gave that time to God. When we set our hearts on things above and give up the things in life that are not good for us, it is one way we show love back to God and I believe He will bless us for that.

LIFE CHALLENGE: Memorize Philippians 4: 8. Analyze how you spend your time (in action and in thoughts) and see if there are any things that you know do not pass this test. These are the things you need to offer up in prayer.

14. Conquering Fear

There was a time in my life when I would only try new activities if someone else tried it with me. I was so concerned with what others thought of me, that I would constantly be anxious about impressing people. I was caught up in trying to be seen doing the "cool" things and hanging out with the cool people. I remember almost every comment made about me, good or bad, and I remember crying at night if I thought someone didn't like me. But the Lord got a hold of my heart and challenged my thinking. "I am your audience. I am the one person whose opinion you should care about," the Lord imprinted on my heart. "Everyone else's opinion does not matter. You should be doing what I have called you to do." As I grew in my relationship with the Lord, I started catching these anxious thoughts of impressing people and bringing them captive to the Lord. I would mentally challenge myself to not worry or fear about what others thought of me, for I had decided I was going to please God, not man.

We all have fears. Fear is very powerful. In the haunting book *1984* by George Orwell, fear was what the Party used to control people. They used fear to keep people obedient to their plans. And in the end, Winston and Julia both succumbed to their fears and returned to their former obedient state. In the same way, our fears directly affect what we will and will not do and just like in *1984*, our fears can run our whole lives, directing our every move, and sometimes limiting our opportunities to serve the Lord and others in amazing ways. Maybe you don't fear what other's think about you or trying something new. Maybe you fear failure or singlehood or marriage. Maybe you fear boredom with life or public speaking. I could think of many more, but you need to really analyze your own heart and see what fears lie there.

What are the fears that trouble your heart?

_____

_____

_____

_____

What do these fears keeping you from doing?

_____

_____

_____

_____

Many times I have had fears of getting involved in certain activities or joining a church group or ministry. I first think several things: • Am I doing the right thing? •Will the people accept me? •Will I make a difference? • Do I really want to give up more of my free time? •Will it be worth it? But once I spend time in prayer about it and know that it is a step of obedience that I need to take, I make up my mind to step out of the boat of human doubt into the sea of faith—just like Peter in Matthew 14:25-31. Of course, once I step away from my time of prayer, the doubts and fears try to sneak their way in and drag me under the water. It is at that moment that one has to remember the confidence one had during the time of prayer regarding the situation and act on that. This brings up the added benefit of journaling. When we are praying in the Word and asking the Lord to reveal a decision to make, we should write down what we feel the Lord is saying to our hearts. Then we have a record of what the Lord told us to do and this will remind us to act on that and not on the fears and doubts.

When I left home to go to college, a good friend of mine, a wise old woman, gave me a Scripture verse to put on my desk. She printed it out on hot pink paper so I would always notice it. It is Joshua 1:9. "Have not I commanded thee? Be strong and of good courage; be not afraid, neither be thou dismayed; for the Lord thy God is with thee whithersoever thou goest." This verse still sits on my desk. It has been a constant reminder to conquer my fear. The words have been an encouragement to me when times were hard and weary. They have helped me out of my dungeon of fear and given me courage to do what needs to be done. And so the Lord has given me little challenges throughout my life, things I felt He was calling me to do that require me to step out in faith. I think back to my hot pink Joshua 1:9 and remind myself, "Is it not God who is commanding me?" When I was given the idea to start a Bible study with people in my grad school, I was so scared that no one would show up. I did not know very many people and I thought that the students would make jokes at the notion of studying the Bible. To my surprise, people came and seemed to enjoy talking about God. And as we dove deeper in the Word and really got to know each other, all my fears turned into gratefulness for what the Lord had allowed me to be a part of. God, the Creator of the Universe, is with me, what have I to fear? Why should I fear anything besides Him?

Read Joshua 1. How many times was Joshua told to "be strong and courageous"?

_____

_____

_____

_____

What I find interesting is that the Lord told Joshua three times to be strong and courageous. He not only gave him clear instructions as to what to do, but He also had to give him courage as well. I'm sure this particular phrase rung in Joshua's ears as he set about making plans. Then as he put the Lord's commands into action, the Lord used the people he was speaking to in order to encouragement him once more. The same phrase "Be strong and courageous" is used by the people in verse 18 when they decide to follow Joshua's leadership. It seems he needed to hear it just one more time or that he needed confirmation somehow. Whatever it was, he received it and continued on implementing his plan.

Are there times in your life when you need that extra encouragement from the Lord? I don't think there is anything wrong with that. But what did Joshua do once he received these words of encouragement? He didn't sit back in idleness. He didn't complain. He didn't wonder what the people were going to think of him. He started getting right to work. That is how we should be too.

What else does the Bible say regarding fear? Read the following verses and write down what our attitude should be regarding fear?

Psalm 27:1-3

_____

_____

Psalm 46:1-7

_____

_____

Psalm 76:7

_____

_____

Proverbs 29:25

_____

_____

Isaiah 51:7,8

We should not fear man. We should not fear man's reproach. Likewise, we should not fear serving the Lord and doing the Lord's will. Psalm 34:4 says, "I sought the Lord and he answered me, he delivered me from all my fears." We should understand that trusting in the Lord removes all our fears. How does God deliver one from their fears? He doesn't magically just take them away from our hearts. Not that He can't, but I think what He would rather have us do is *step out in faith first*. Then as we see how the Lord is working and supporting us, we will gain confidence in what we are doing and the fear will depart.

LIFE CHALLENGE: Make a list of two or three things that fear is keeping you from doing. Offer these up in prayer to the Lord and write down how the Lord answers you. Then go out in faith and obedience! See how the Lord will provide and will be with you along the way! If you don't, you will never know what you may be missing out on! Don't forget to write down how the Lord removed your fears and gave you confidence!

15. FRIENDSHIPS

Here is a little analogy on friendship. I am the gardener of my friendship garden. You are the gardener of your friendship garden. When you plant the seeds, you must make sure each type of plant gets planted into the proper soil and obtains the sunlight condition that is most beneficial for its growth. In other words, each friendship is a little different. Some are lima beans—extremely easy to grow, rising tall and maturing quickly, producing lots of fruit throughout the year. Some are tomatoes—easy to grow as long as you fertilize them periodically. Some are lantanas that grow quickly and form what's called a "monoculture" by keeping other plants from growing and prospering— they want the whole garden to themselves. Some are orchids that require tender care and very specific environmental conditions in order to bloom.

Each plant takes root in different environments and each personality gives and receives love in different ways. As the gardener, you must make sure each seed gets what is best for it. The gardener must water on a regular basis, for very few plants can maintain growth and productivity with an inconsistent water supply. Water to plants is communication to friendships. As you water, the seed will respond and eventually grow roots in order to position itself in the soil and obtain nutrients. Soon, it will start to produce small leaves and a stem, eventually growing taller and stronger. If the gardener continues to supply water, the plant should end up producing fruit and all the labor is rewarded. But since each plant is different, they will produce fruit depending on their individual harvest times, so patience may be required. But this fruit/blossom is the finale! It is the Great Reward! It gives mutual satisfaction and edification for both the plant and the gardener and it is worth waiting for!

Sometimes, even with water and tender loving care, the plant will not produce fruit. There are several possibilities. Maybe it just requires something a little extra to get it going. This extra might be some fertilizer to provide just the right conditions for the plant to take off and bloom. Fertilizers come in several ratios of carbon, nitrogen, and phosphorus and in the same way, friendships can require different types of interactions to get them to bloom. For instance, one person's primary love language may not be in verbal communication, but may be gifts or acts of service. Therefore, to get this friendship to deepen and produce fruit, doing something for the person or spending some quality time with the person may be exactly what is needed for the doors of fruitfulness to open up. (For more on love languages, read Gary Chapman's book *The Five Love Languages*).

Even with extra special attention and fertilizer, a plant may still whither. This is a hard thing for the gardener to understand. You have done all you can do to resuscitate it, but it continues to drop leaves and withers away with each passing day. You may feel dejected by the plant or disappointed in the plant's outcome. Unsure of what is causing the failure, sometimes you can't help but assume that you are at fault. Yet, it could be due to some pesky critter or weed that worked its way into your garden. If you examine carefully, you may notice the scars of beetles, mites, fungus, or aphids. Any of these can destroy the potential of a promising plant. Weeds can also come in and choke the life out of a plant. These pests are things like pride, unforgiveness, jealousy, worldly distractions, apathy, and other sins that will negatively affect a friendship. If you can treat the problem with pesticide/herbicide (prayer, God's Word, patience, and love), then maybe the plant will come back. If it is too late, the plant dies regardless of the application of pesticide. The heart of the plant has become hardened and ugly. One sad day it will need to be removed from the garden—especially if the disease is contagious. In order to prevent the pest from affecting other plants, it must be removed, as well as all traces of the disease/pest. It will become just a memory in the mind of the gardener.

Not all pests are visible from above ground either. Some pests work their way into the soil and eat the roots of the plant. The gardener might never see these coming and though all efforts are made to resuscitate the plant, it still withers away into nothingness. Only the plant itself knows the type of pest that is causing its failing health. Another reason why some of the plants in the garden may fail or not be very productive is that other plants may grow up quicker and taller and shade the smaller plants from the sun that they need. The small plant will still survive, but will never reach its peak productivity unless its environmental conditions are changed for its benefit. As the gardener, it is important that you notice if the plants are getting the right amount of sunlight and water. If you notice that one plant is not receiving the right amount of sun, try moving its location to a place that is a perfect fit for what it requires. Then it should be productive and grateful for the constant care and attention of its gardener.

One day, as you walk through the garden, you might notice that growing in a corner that you barely attend to is a beautiful surprise. A perfect rose growing in a place you did not even plant a seed. You stop in your tracks and examine the flower. A big smile breaks across your face as you realize how lovely it is. It smells wonderful and its fragrance is strong and comforting. You wonder how this beautiful plant came to this spot, especially with so little attention from you. It is at that moment that you realize it is a gift from the Master Gardener. He planted it when you least noticed and the rains of heaven tenderly nourished that bush and made it into something you never could have planned on nor dreamed of how its beauty would affect your heart. Now as you walk through the garden, that rose is one of the first things you notice. It brings you so much joy and encouragement, for it reminds you of the Master's love. The surprise roses are those friendships that come directly from God's intervention in our lives: the ones we did not plan on, but just happened without the least amount of effort from us. These seem to be the most rewarding and encouraging. They make the garden less work and more peaceful and enjoyable. These are true gifts.

How is your friendship garden? In other words, are you actively involved in friendships?

_____

_____

_____

_____

    There are many people in this world who believe that they are perfectly fine being alone and without friends. Yet, that is not what God intended for us. He created us to be able to fellowship with others.

What do these verses say about the benefit of friendships?

Proverbs 17:17

_____

_____

Proverbs 27:6

_____

_____

Proverbs 27:9

_____

_____

Proverbs 27:17

_____

_____

Ecclesiastes 4:10

A friend is someone you can count on to encourage your spirit when you are down. A friend will lift you up when you fall and help set you back on the right path. A friend will sharpen you and challenge you to be a better person. A friend will give you counsel when you need it. A friend will make your heart merry and pleasant. The benefits of friendship go on and on. Of course, Jesus modeled the perfect friendship and so we know the depths of love a friend should have for others (John 15:13). As women, we were created to be full of emotions that men may never understand. There are depths to a woman's soul that cannot be explained with words. And so there is a chasm that emotionally sets us apart from men. That is why friendship is so important.

Fellowship is a word commonly used in Scripture. It implies something deeper and more intimate than a cordial gathering together. It is a sharing of common interests, common desires, common prayers, and common struggles. It implies unity with a motivation to lift each other up with real agape love for each other. That is what God intended when he told Christians to gather together and be unified.

Read 1 John 1:1-7 and note how many times fellowship is mentioned. So again I ask, how is your friendship garden? How are you at being the gardener?

An elderly missionary woman wrote me a letter on friendship when I was struggling with a friendship. Her words have forever been imprinted in my mind. "It is better to be a friend than to have a friend." And so I changed my selfish attitude to one of servanthood in trying to be a friend, regardless of the attitude on the receiving end. And wouldn't you know, while I thought that was the end of the friendship, a few years later, I received a letter where she apologized for her attitude and complemented me on how good of a friend I

Danielle J Londeree

was. It goes to show that the Lord will bless your endeavors to build friendships, no matter how hard the gardening may be.

PRAYER CHALLENGE: Make a list of your trusted friends. Pray for each of them today and thank the Lord for them. A good prayer to pray for them is Ephesians 1:15 – 18.

LIFE CHALLENGE: Examine your friendships. Are there friends with whom you need to be keep in better touch? Are there friends that you need to encourage and pray for more often? If you don't have any Christian friends that you can fellowship with, please consider joining a Bible Study or women's group at a church. I think you will be pleasantly surprised by the roses God may plant in your garden.

16. WHOLE-HEARTED DEVOTION

What is wholehearted devotion? Webster defines it as fully or completely sincere, enthusiastic, and energetic. So how energetic and enthusiastic are you about the Lord? How sincere is your trust and faith in Him? There are many wonderful biblical examples of individuals who followed after God wholeheartedly. They will help us see wholehearted devotion put into action. We will first examine King David. God described him as a "man after His own heart" (1 Sam. 13:14). I take this phrase to mean two things: 1) David understood the Lord's heart like no other and 2) he searched and followed hard after it. Since he understood the Lord so well, we get a chance to hear some advice and insight into this matter. The following passages take place when David is handing over the kingdom to his son Solomon.

In doing so, He gave some very important details as to how to please God. What does he say?

1 Chronicles 28:8-10

_____

_____

1 Kings 2:1-4

There are some key things to observe in these passages as David describes what a life devoted to God looks like. You will acknowledge Him, follow all of His commands carefully, and serve Him with two things: your heart and your willing mind. Why? Because God searches every heart and understands them. There is nothing you can hide from Him. He sees your thoughts and knows the motives behind your every action. It is not just deeds He cares about (and therefore you might get away with some superficial actions of obedience). He wants your whole heart and mind to be in devotion to Him! In addition, there is a promise given: if you seek Him, you *will* find Him, but if you reject Him, He *will* reject you. All of our seeking after the Lord will not be in vain. He will reveal Himself to us. King Josiah is another example of one whose heart was devoted to the Lord.

Read 2 Kings 22 – 23:30 to see what was so special about Josiah's reign. What specific things did he do to show his wholehearted devotion to God?

We don't have actual Asherah poles to tear down (at least I hope not), but we can examine our hearts to see what other "gods" we are serving so we can tear them down. When God gave plans of the Temple to David for Solomon to build, it was described as the Lord's resting place, sanctuary, and dwelling place (Deut. 12:1-5, 1 Chron. 22:17-22; 2 Chron. 5:13-6:2, 40-42). But when Christ died for our sins, our bodies became the new temple of the Lord (1 Cor. 3:16; 6:19-20; 2 Cor. 6:16)! Can these same descriptions also be used to describe your heart? Is your heart really the Lord's resting place? Or is He never at rest because He is constantly battling against other kings (pride, money, beauty, success, knowledge, chocolate, coffee, TV, selfish ambition, etc.) vying for the throne? We need to remove these "Asherah shrines" from our hearts and give God the Throne.

List some other kings (idols, gods) that are fighting for reign in your heart. Ask the Lord to remove them from your heart so you can love Him whole-heartedly.

_____

_____

_____

What does Jesus say concerning the conditions of the heart in the following passages?

Matthew 6:21

_____

_____

Matthew 22:34-40

_____

_____

In summary, we can only have *one* master over our hearts. We need to love God with all of our heart, our mind, our soul, and strength. This is what the Lord truly desires of us. This is what pleases Him greatly and this should be our goal. If we truly believe that God will satisfy all our desires so that there is no need to give the throne over to another, what will our lives look like?

Tozer has an interesting way of describing the relinquishing of our hearts over to Christ. He describes it as, "The Blessedness of Possessing Nothing." He discusses the story of Abraham in the Bible and how God tested his heart to see who was really reigning on the throne. Read Genesis 22 for the complete story. Tozer goes on to examine Abraham's relationship with his son. His son was the delight of his heart and represented all the dreams and hopes Abraham had for the future of his family. But God sensed Abraham's love for his son rivaled the throne of Abraham's heart. Who knows if/how Abraham's own relationship with God may have gradually waned as Isaac grew older, but at some point, God decided to test him. We can only imagine all the turmoil and pain Abraham was going through during this trip to Moriah with his son. Yet at the end, the only peace he received was when he trusted God to raise Isaac from the dead (Heb. 11:17-19). It was then that he was ready to remove Isaac from his throne, for he remembered God's promises. It is at that moment that Tozer describes Abraham as "a man utterly obedient, a man who possessed nothing." Tozer continues.

We are often hindered from giving up our treasures to the Lord out of fear for their safety. This is especially true when those treasured are loved relatives and friends. But we need have no such fears. Our Lord came not to destroy but to save. Everything is safe which we commit to Him, and nothing is safe which is not so committed. Our gifts and talents should also be turned over to Him. They should be recognized by what they are, God's loan to us, and should never be considered in any sense our own.

The blessedness of possessing nothing is one of the best lessons I have learned. I often reread that chapter in Tozer's book and remind myself that everything I have is the Lord's, including my relationships with others. Understanding this has freed me from worry, from getting upset when something happens to "my" car or to "my" house or to "my" family. There was a time when I was dating my husband that I realized our relationship was on the throne of my heart. I would often fret over his safety if I didn't hear from him or I would plan my whole life—including my spiritual life—around when we would be together. When we broke up for a brief time period, I experienced a grief and pain that I had never experienced before. It was then that God tested me in the same way he tested Abraham. I learned so much during that time period. I learned to trust God with my heart in a way that I had never done before. I learned many of His promises and would remember them whenever

I would feel disheartened or worried. I desired to follow hard after Him regardless of my own hopes and fears.

Take a moment and envision what a life would look like for the one who fully trusts God wholeheartedly. What would be evident in her life?

_____

_____

_____

_____

I envision a woman who never complains about anything because she is fully satisfied. She understands that complaining about life is the same as complaining about God's will for her life. She always receives the trials in her life with joy. She does not worry about tomorrow, but puts her hopes and fears in the hands of the Savior. She does not let her emotions control her life, but remembers to be still before the Lord throughout the day. She readily accepts her responsibilities in life and seeks the Lord's will over her own plans, regardless of her dreams and desires. She always prays before making decisions and has confidence in putting them into action, without procrastination. This is my vision of what a life would look like with a heart that fully trusts in the Lord. This to me is loving the Lord with all your heart, mind, soul, and strength (Matt. 22:37).

I have reread my vision over and over. Sometimes I cry because I know how far I am from being that woman. Yet my soul longs for it just as the deer pants for water. Many times I have been on my knees begging the Lord to change me into that vision in an instant. But the Lord just smiles at me and reminds me that it is a process. We will travel the journey hand in hand together, but there are no short-cuts. When I get down, He sends me encouragement—from friends, family, church, the Word, prayer, and butterflies—when I need it. He also grants me a renewed heart on a regular basis. Every day I feel like I gain the strength to become that woman.

Now that you have your vision, how can you implement changes in your own life so this vision can become a reality? What two or three things can you do to trust the Lord with your heart and make Him your daily spiritual bread?

_____

_____

_____

_____

If you can't come up with anything, here are some ideas that work for me. My first recommendation would be to start memorizing Scripture on this subject or keep some of the verses from the previous sections written on note cards and carry them with you throughout the day. I tend to write verses on pretty paper and stick them on a wall in a room where I spend a lot of time. It reminds me to focus my attention on the Lord, especially when frustrating situations come my way or I get disappointed in people or myself. For example, Philippians 2:14 reminds me to "do everything without complaining or arguing."

My second recommendation would be to start journaling your heartfelt emotions, desires, prayers, and struggles to the Lord. As you write your "letters to God," as I call them, you will find that the Lord will begin to change your heart and give you peace. Journaling also teaches you to be honest before the Lord and helps you see how the Lord is working in situations as you record your prayers over time. It will also hopefully get you in the habit of spending time with God on an intimate level.

LIFE CHALLENGE: If you don't already have one, purchase a journal and get to work writing your heart out before the Lord. Write down your vision of a woman whose heart is fully devoted to her Lord on the first page.

17. CALLED TO PERSEVERE INTO RIGHTEOUSNESS

Well, have you become the vision you wrote down last chapter?

No?

I'm going to shock you here, but it might take more than a day or two. It might take months or years. Sorry to disappoint you, but its true. It's a journey that we walk every day, but hopefully we are always walking forward! It's a journey that takes perseverance! Scripture talks often about perseverance. It gives it utmost importance and often describes blessings for those who persevere to the end of their life and curses for those who choose not to.

What do the following verses say about perseverance? What specific rewards are there?

Romans 5:1-5

_____

_____

Hebrews 10:35-39

_____

_____

Hebrews 12:1-3

_____

_____

James 1:12

_____

_____

_____

2 Peter 1:3-11

_____

_____

The rewards of perseverance are blessings, honor, riches in glory, and salvation (this could mean salvation from evils on this earth or from God's wrath). What is also interesting to note is that perseverance will produce godliness. What this means is that as we persevere (to continue getting up after our falls, staying strong in our faith and convictions), we will eventually become more godly and will display the character of Christ. All it takes is perseverance. Remember back to the previous chapters on choosing to get up and walk again? That's a big part of what it means to persevere.

In reference to the passage in 2 Peter, Oswald Chambers states, "*Add* means there is something we have to do. . . . No man is born either naturally or supernaturally with character, he has to make character. Nor are we born with habits, we have to form habits on the basis of the new life God has put in us."[6] In other words, we have to choose to develop godly habits (it is not going to happen without our intervention) and actually act out these traits so that it becomes habit. Then eventually you will lose the consciousness that you are performing a habit at all. That is the goal! That is when you have reached true Christ-like character where your actions are so intertwined with love for the Lord that you are not consciously choosing the right path, but are just living in love.

What godly habits do you need to initiate in your life?

_____

_____

_____

_____

_____

How can you start practicing these traits?

_____

_____

_____

_____

_____

For example, if I wanted to develop the habit of being thankful in all circumstances, then there are several actions I can start doing on a regular basis so that it will become a habit.

1. I can memorize several verses on thankfulness or keep them posted in places I often need reminders to be grateful (office wall, car, closet, bathroom mirror).
2. I can start writing down things to be thankful for in a journal.
3. I can develop the habit of writing people thank-you notes, even for little things or for just being a part of my life.
4. I can spend a few minutes every night thinking through the day and thanking God for things, no matter how frustrating or disappointing the day was – remember he always works for the good of those He calls (Romans 8:28).

Now make your own list of how to practice the traits you mentioned. Maybe starting off with one trait would be less overwhelming. Then once that trait is a habit, make another list for another trait.

_____

_____

_____

_____

One godly trait I have been trying for years—practically my whole life—to incorporate into my life is to spend *daily quality* time with the Lord. Sometimes I have no problem with the daily part and sometimes I have no problem with the quality part, but it's getting the two of them together that seems to be the hard part. I recently looked back on my journals in high school and college and read about how I was going to make a habit of devoting some deep, character building time to God every day. But the cycle continues. Yet the lesson I keep learning is this: persevere! Every so often, I feel guilty for not having deep, intimate quiet times with the Lord. I get back on my knees and ask the Lord again to develop this habit with me, and I know He blesses me for trying. Yet, I know that one day, I will overcome—or at least not cycle so many times—as long as I persevere. It's the perseverance that matters! Don't give up!

LIFE CHALLENGE: If you don't already have a consistent intimate alone time with the Lord, try waking earlier (at least 15 to 20 minutes earlier than you usually do) and go sit with the Lord. This one habit alone can dramatically change your heart because it requires putting God first in the morning. Just this act shows how devoted you are your Maker and I believe He will reward you for making Him the first person you talk to every day!

Endnotes

1. Tozer, AW. 1993. *Pursuit of God*. Camp Hill, PA: Christian Publications.

2. Snider, Julie. July 29,2004. A Body of Work. USA Today.

3. Doup, Liz. May 29, 2005. The Beauty Frontier. Sun Sentinel.

4. Kirchheimer, Sid. September 12, 2003. WebMD Medical News.

5. Tozer, AW. 1997. *The Attributes of God Volume One with Study Guide*. Camp Hill, PA: Christian Publications

6. Chambers, Oswald. 1963. *My Utmost for His Highest*. Uhrichsville, OH: Barbour and Company.